Facts About Blue Catfish

By Lisa Strattin

© 2016 Lisa Strattin

Facts for Kids Picture Books by Lisa Strattin

Ladybugs and Fireflies, Vol 1

Squids Will Be Squids, Vol 2

What Are Manx Cats, Vol 3

Dirty Boys, Why Bathe, Vol 4

Facts About Chipmunks, Vol 5

Firefighters: Help Kids Deal With Death, Vol 6

Facts About Hummingbirds, Vol 7

Facts About African Elephants, Vol 8

Facts About Alligators, Vol 9

Texas Armadillo, Vol 10

Sign Up for New Release Emails Here

http://lisastrattin.com/subscribe-here

Join the KidCrafts Monthly Program Here

http://kidcraftsbylisa.com/

All rights reserved. No part of this book may be reproduced by any means whatsoever without the written permission from the author, except brief portions quoted for purpose of review.

All information in this book has been carefully researched and checked for factual accuracy. However, the author and publisher makes no warranty, express or implied, that the information contained herein is appropriate for every individual, situation or purpose and assume no responsibility for errors or omissions. The reader assumes the risk and full responsibility for all actions, and the author will not be held responsible for any loss or damage, whether consequential, incidental, special or otherwise, that may result from the information presented in this book.

I have relied on my own observations as well as many different sources for this book and I have done my best to check facts and give credit where it is due. In the event that any material is used without proper permission, please contact me so that the oversight can be corrected.

Contents

INTRODUCTION 7
SIZE AND CHARACTERISTICS 9
LIFE STAGES AND LIFE SPAN 11
HABITATS AND HABITS 13
DIET 17
COMMON BEHAVIOR WITH OTHER ANIMALS 19
AS PETS 21
BLUE CATFISH PLUSH TOY 25
KIDCRAFTS MONTHLY SUBSCRIPTION PROGRAM 26

COLOR ME

INTRODUCTION

Blue catfish are also known as Ictalurus Furcatus, this is the combination of two Greek and Latin words, Ictalurus referred to Fish Cat and Latin word Furcatus means forked. It is one of the largest species of Northern American Catfish and if famous due to the forked tail and cat style moustaches as well. It is specifically termed as blue due to blue shading of black and while that give her a plain and stunning but attractive look. Usually it is blue on the back with white shading on the belly, it simply have made the balance contrast in its appearance.

COLOR ME

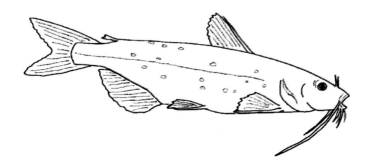

SIZE AND CHARACTERISTICS

The average length of Blue Catfish is 64cm to 117 cm but ultimately it could reach till the 165 cm and could gain the weight of 68 kg that is around 150 lb. there are typically 30 to 35 rays in anal fin of the blue catfish that makes it different from the others in the specie. An experienced eye could simply witness the major difference of the fin rays and could identify the blue catfish among all others due to the.

COLOR ME

LIFE STAGES AND LIFE SPAN

The life of a catfish is around 20 years in which it could reach to its maximum size but still there is a record to break by the dives on finding the estimated long and heavy blue catfish under water. The younger blue catfishes are hatched in about one week and after that the male cat fish will guard them for at least a week. During that week the infants are dependent on the elder one for food after that they are free to swim in water but to a limited scale and have small aquatic animals as diet. Once a blue catfish reaches the size of 24 inches it becomes sexually mature and bring the life cycle on.

COLOR ME

HABITATS AND HABITS

Blue Catfish is the cold water fish that loves to be in the cold water in the larger rivers, in summers it swims towards the up streams in order to get a cool stream. In the winter season it stays in the depth of water to have a warmer feeling and to avoid too much cold around in the environment. Migration according to the seasons and environmental conditions is common in blue catfish. Generally, it could be found in Mississippi River Drainage followed by Missouri, Ohio, Tennessee and Arkansas Rivers. Moreover, to that it could be found in Gulf Coast to Belize and Guatemala. Apart from that you could track down the Blue Catfish in the lakes of Lake Marion, Lake Moultrie at South Carolina, in Virginia James River is popular in having them. In Pkein, Powcr ton Lake, Illinois and Springfield Lake are also occupied by the blue catfish in Springfield, Illinois.

COLOR ME

There is not a specified region where you can locate them in fact it is not hard for you to have glimpse of this amazing creature. The fish is also found in the Florida lakes easily all around the year. Moving to the habits of blue catfish then it seems to be like a calm and relaxed fish that make movement easily according to the needs but when there is any threat to life or the family then aggression comes in action.

COLOR ME

DIET

Blue Catfish is not a selective one when it is about diet, it could have anything that is firstly available to it like an opportunistic predator. The blue catfishes eat any specie that they can catch easily under deep water or at the upper scale as well. Along with other fishes they do prey mussel, frogs, crawfish and other available aquatic animals. They are very much reflexive towards the freshly dead or wounded prey they are famous for feeding on the wounded bait fishes that are washed through power generation turbines or dams. There were some attacked reported by the Blue catfishes on scuba divers under sea water. The younger blue catfish feed on small fishes and aquatic insects in the beginning and later on match up with the elder ones.

COLOR ME

COMMON BEHAVIOR WITH OTHER ANIMALS

Generally, the Blue Fish is considered as the powerful one, once it gets into fight it takes it to the next level on the basis of its determination and strength as well. Due to the power and strength and focus on fight it makes sure that the opponent will bit the dust and it could win it for sure. Whenever a blue catfish is in action with an angler it is a worth watching fight that makes things warmer around. Under water most of the aquatic residents do not want to get messed with the blue catfish. As a whole if we have a look over the environmental coordination of blue catfish then it seems to be normal and pleasant that is not really a hard one for the other present there. But, when it is about hunting for food then blue catfish is in complete aggression and do not want to let the bait go off.

COLOR ME

AS PETS

Blue catfish is a free fish that loves to get adjusted in the environmental conditions according to the weather and other surroundings too. But, if you plan up to have it as a pet then it is really a big challenge for you. Once it is large enough that you could not have it as pet at your place you need a huge setup for that. On the other hand, although you can find out the blue cat fish easily around in the fresh lakes and larger rivers but catching it is a different thing and a big thing as well. There is a lot of expertise is required in that so it will be hard on you. It is really not the animal that is good with being a pet in fact it is a free one that likes to move under water freely and openly so it will be a bad thought in keeping the blue cat fish as pet.

COLOR ME

Please leave me a review here:

http://lisastrattin.com/Review-Vol-17

For more Kindle Downloads Visit Lisa Strattin Author Page on Amazon Author Central

http://amazon.com/author/lisastrattin

To see upcoming titles, visit my website at LisaStrattin.com – all books available on kindle!

http://lisastrattin.com

BLUE CATFISH PLUSH TOY

You can get one by copying and pasting this link into your browser: http://lisastrattin.com/catfishtoy

KIDCRAFTS MONTHLY SUBSCRIPTION PROGRAM

Receive a Box of Crafts and a Lisa Strattin Full Color Paperback Book Each Month in Your Mailbox!

Get yours by copying and pasting this link into your browser

http://KidCraftsByLisa.com

Made in the USA
Lexington, KY
20 January 2018